MW01227788

118440 EN   598 PAR PAR
Birds

Parker, Janice
B.L.: 4.3
Points: 0.5   LG

LIFE SCIENCE

BIRDS

Janice Parker

WEIGL PUBLISHERS INC.

Project Coordinator
Heather C. Hudak

Design
Bryan Pezzi

Cover Design
Terry Paulhus

Published by Weigl Publishers Inc.
350 5th Avenue, Suite 3304, PMB 6G
New York, NY 10118-0069

Website: www.weigl.com
Copyright ©2008 WEIGL PUBLISHERS INC.
All rights reserved. No part of this publication may be reproduced,
stored in a retrieval system, or transmitted in any form or by any
means, electronic, mechanical, photocopying, recording, or otherwise,
without the prior written permission of the publisher.

All of the Internet URLs given in the book were valid at the time of
publication. However, due to the dynamic nature of the Internet, some
addresses may have changed, or sites may have ceased to exist since
publication. While the author and publisher regret any inconvenience
this may cause readers, no responsibility for any such changes can be
accepted by either the author or the publisher.

Library of Congress Cataloging-in-Publication Data

Parker, Janice.
  Birds / Janice Parker.
    p. cm. -- (Life science)
  Includes index.
  ISBN 978-1-59036-703-2 (hard cover : alk. paper) -- ISBN 978-1-
59036-704-9 (soft cover : alk. paper)
  1. Birds--Juvenile literature. I. Title.
  QL676.2.P363 2008
  598--dc22

                    2007012617

Printed in the United States of America
1 2 3 4 5 6 7 8 9 0 11 10 09 08 07

Every reasonable effort has been made to trace ownership and to
obtain permission to reprint copyright material. The publishers would
be pleased to have any errors or omissions brought to their attention
so that they may be corrected in subsequent printings.

Contents

What Do You Know about Birds? 4

Life Cycles 6

Feet and Bills 8

Types of Birds 10

Working with Birds 12

Birds and People 14

Our Feathered Friends 16

Habitat 18

Avoiding Danger 20

Building a Nest 22

Web of Life 24

Protecting Birds 26

Singing is for the Birds 28

The First Bird 30

Glossary 32

Index 32

Websites 32

What Do You Know about Birds?

Birds are a type of animal. Mammals, reptiles, **amphibians**, fish, and insects are other types of animals. Birds are vertebrates. This means they have a backbone. Many different **species** of birds live in the world. All birds share similar features and habits.

Most birds fly, but some birds cannot. All birds lay eggs. They all have bills. Other animals share some of these features with birds.

■ **The hummingbird was given its name because of the humming sound its wings make.**

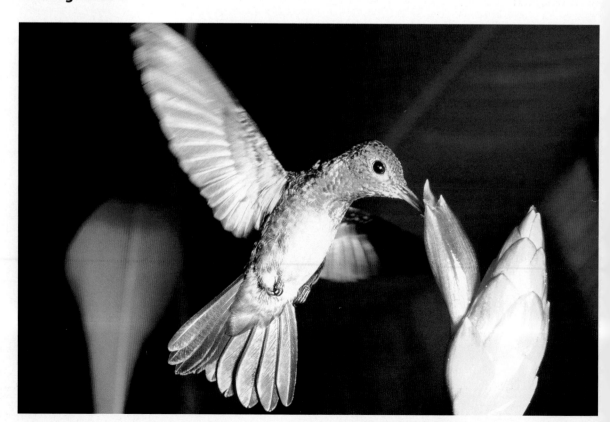

4

However, all birds have one feature that no other animal has—feathers. Other animals may be covered in fur, hair, or scales, but never in feathers. Whether or not a bird can fly, it has feathers covering its body.

Macaws are large parrots. They have brightly colored feathers and long, pointed tails.

Puzzler

Name all the birds you can think of that cannot fly. How many can you identify?

Answer: Cassowaries, emus, kiwis, ostriches, and penguins are examples of flightless birds.

Life Cycles

All plants and animals have a life cycle. They all begin life, grow, **reproduce**, and die. Like all other living things, birds have a life

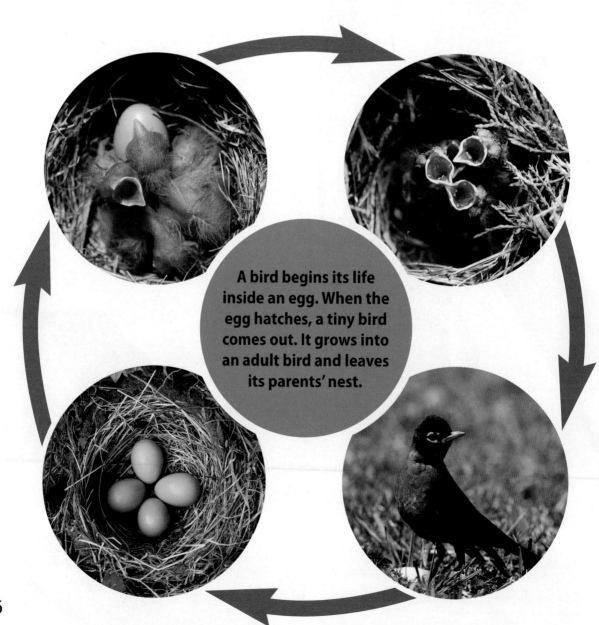

A bird begins its life inside an egg. When the egg hatches, a tiny bird comes out. It grows into an adult bird and leaves its parents' nest.

Some birds are blind and without feathers when they hatch out of their eggs. They must rely on their parents for food and protection. Other birds are able to live on their own soon after hatching.

When young birds are strong enough, they leave their parents to start their own lives. They will mate and have baby birds of their own.

Puzzler

Why are some types of birds ready to leave the nest earlier than others?

Answer: When a baby bird decides to leave the nest depends on its parents. Some types of bird parents give very little care to the young birds once they have hatched. These baby birds must be able to feed themselves quickly. Other types of bird parents stay with their young for weeks or months.

7

Feet and Bills

To keep track of the many different types of birds, scientists group them by their features. Feet and bills are an easy way to tell the difference between birds. The feet and bills can tell us what a bird eats and in what type of area it lives.

Types of Feet and Bills

A goose's large, webbed feet work like paddles in the water.

A sparrow uses its perching feet to stand on branches.

A flamingo's bill picks up the tiny plants that the bird eats from the water.

An owl's strong feet help the bird grasp its **prey**.

An ostrich's feet are designed for running and carrying the bird's heavy body.

Activity

Looking at Birds

Search through magazines and books for photographs of birds. Look at the birds' bills and feet. Try to decide what types of food the birds might eat or where they might live.

A pelican's bill allows the bird to scoop up fish.

A pigeon's bill makes it easy for the bird to pick up small seeds and fruit.

An eagle's bill works like a knife to tear the bird's prey.

A parrot's strong bill can crack nuts and fruits.

A hummingbird's bill is long. The bird can put its bill deep into large flowers to collect **nectar**.

Types of Birds

Nearly 9,000 species of birds exist in the world. Scientists put every bird in one of 27 groups, or orders. Birds in the same order have similar features.

Types of Birds

Birds of Prey	Perching Birds	Hummingbirds and Swifts	Owls
• eat other animals • excellent flyers	• biggest group of birds • feet are designed for grasping branches • live over land	• often live in tropical **habitats** • strong, fast fliers • very small	• eat other animals • more than 140 different types • usually hunt at night
Examples eagle, falcon, osprey	**Examples** blue jay, chickadee, swallow	**Examples** chimney swift, ruby-throated hummingbird	**Examples** hawk o screech owl, snowy

Puzzler

To which group does the crow belong?

Answer: Crows belong in the perching group. They live over land and are related to blue jays.

Penguins	Pigeons and Doves	Waterfowl	Ostrich
• 17 different types • live in warm and cold habitats • swim well	• feathers are stiff and smooth • have a plump body • live all over the world	• build nests near bodies of water • dive underwater to find food • webbed feet	• flightless • largest bird • only bird in its group
Examples chinstrap, emperor, Galápagos	**Examples** crowned pigeon, inca dove, mourning dove	**Examples** mute swan, snow goose, wood duck	**Examples** ostrich

Working with Birds

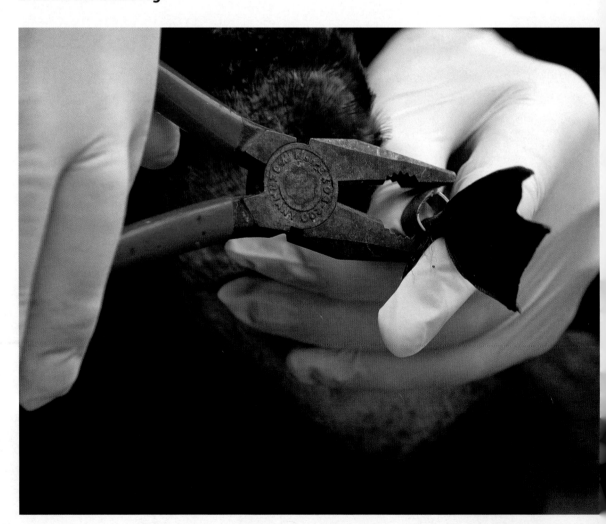

I f you love birds, you may want to get a job where you can work with them. Many types of careers involve birds. Zookeepers, biologists, and **poultry** farmers all may work with birds. Ornithology is the study of birds.

■ If scientists want to keep track of a bird, they carefully place a small, metal identification tag around the bird's leg.

Ornithologists work to learn more about birds. They also try to help save **endangered** birds. In order to become an ornithologist, you have to study the science of animals at a university. Even if you do not work with birds, you can still be a bird-watcher. There are many bird-watching clubs around the world.

■ Many zoos have a bird sanctuary, where parrots and other birds are given large, open spaces for flying.

■ Turkeys are raised on poultry farms.

Activity

Bird-watching

Go outdoors, and see how many different types of birds you can spot. If possible, bring binoculars and a book with pictures and names of birds that live in your area. Bring a pencil and paper to write down what you see. Note where and when you saw a bird.

Birds and People

Birds are important to humans for many different reasons. People sometimes keep birds, such as canaries, as pets. Many birds are quite happy to live with people.

Some people love to watch birds in nature. These bird-watchers will often go out into the wilderness early in the morning, hoping to see certain birds. Bird-watchers often make lists of the different birds they have seen. Over time, some bird-watchers might see hundreds of different types of birds.

■ Parrots are great pets. They can learn to mimic, or copy, sounds and words.

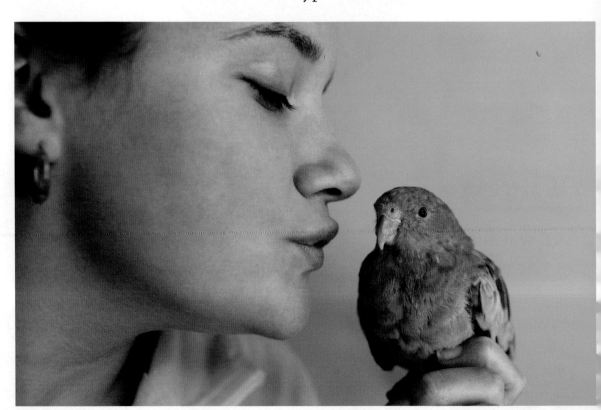

Bird feathers can be used in clothing and other items. Many homes have pillows or comforters that are filled with feathers and down. Down is especially good at keeping people warm. The warmest jackets and sleeping bags often contain down.

People eat certain kinds of birds, such as turkey, chicken, duck, or goose. Many people eat chickens' eggs.

The Ukrainian culture values Easter eggs as symbols of spring and new life. The eggs are decorated with traditional Ukrainian designs.

Activity

Looking at Eggs

Crack a chicken's egg into a dish. Look closely at the shell. An eggshell protects growing birds from the outside world. Eggshells are quite strong. The yellow part of the egg is called the **yolk**. If a young bird lived in the egg, it would eat the yolk as it grew. The clear part of the egg is called the egg white, or **albumen**. The albumen protects the growing bird. It also provides the bird with liquid and vitamins.

Our Feathered Friends

Birds have different kinds and colors of feathers. A small bird, such as a hummingbird, may have only 1,000 feathers. A large bird, such as a swan, may have more than 25,000. Most birds have four different types of feathers. Down feathers are the soft ones close to the bird's body. These feathers help keep the bird warm. Most of the bird is covered with body feathers. Tail feathers help the bird keep its balance. Tail feathers are often used to help attract mates. Wing feathers help a bird fly or move around.

wing feathers

body feathers

tail feathers

■ Baby birds are usually covered in down feathers.

Most feathers have four parts. The shaft is the stiff, stick-like section in the middle of the feather. Vanes are attached to the shaft. Barbs are attached to the vanes. Tiny barbules come out from the barbs.

Birds spend a great deal of time **preening** their feathers. Combing through feathers with their beaks helps keep the feathers oiled and working well.

Activity

A Close Look at Feathers

Try to find a feather from any type of bird. Place the feather on a light-colored piece of paper. Look closely at the feather. Can you see the barbs? Is the feather flat and shiny or soft and fluffy? Try to guess which type of bird the feather came from.

Habitat

Birds live all over the world. They live in tropical forests and in hot deserts. Some live at sea. Some even live in the cold polar regions. Birds can live in such various habitats because they have adapted to them. Different types of birds have developed special features that help them live in different environments.

Cliff dwellers

have adapted to living and laying eggs on the edges of steep cliffs. The murre does not make a nest. It lays its eggs on a ledge. The eggs are pointy at one end. If a murre egg is knocked around, it will roll in circles, like a top. The egg will not roll off the ledge.

Arctic birds

have adapted to living in cold, snowy areas. The snowy owl's white feathers help it hide from its prey. The feet of snowy owls are covered by soft, warm feathers that look like fur.

Puzzler

In what ways is the penguin adapted to swimming?

Answer: The penguin's body shape helps it move easily through water. Penguin wings work like rudders to help the bird change direction while swimming. The feet are webbed and work like paddles. The penguin's body is covered in shiny, waterproof feathers that dry quickly.

Wading birds

have adapted to living near lakes, streams, and marshes. The crowned crane has very long legs. This lets the bird wander through water in search of food.

Water birds

have adapted to swimming and taking off from water. Swans have large, webbed feet. These feet are shaped like paddles and help the swan swim. A swan's long neck allows it to dip its head under water to search for food.

City birds

have adapted to living near people. Some, such as pigeons and crows, will eat almost anything people feed them. They are not shy around people.

Avoiding Danger

■ Can you tell which mallard duck is female and which is male?

Most birds have ways to avoid becoming another animal's dinner. **Camouflage** helps many birds avoid being caught and eaten. Often, a bird can be heard in a tree but cannot be seen. In many bird species, the female bird is a dull, spotted color, while the male is more colorful. This keeps the female well hidden when she sits on her nest.

Many birds' eggs are camouflaged. Terns lay their eggs on the ground in a nest made of stones. The eggs are spotted and dull in color. They look just like the surrounding stones. The large eggs of an emu are a dark green color. The emu lays its eggs in dark green grasses.

Many birds simply fly away to avoid danger. Only a fast animal can catch a bird if it takes flight. Owls eat other birds. They can catch other birds by surprising them. Owls quickly and quietly swoop down and grab their prey.

A robin's eggs are a light blue color that is easy to see in the nest. Why do you think they are so colorful?

Answer: The adult robin stays on its nest covering the eggs. The eggs are almost always hidden by the parent. If the robin does leave the nest, the egg color might help it find the nest again quickly.

21

Building a Nest

Most birds build nests. Nests are like cradles for the eggs and young birds. Nests come in many shapes and sizes. Hummingbirds are the smallest birds in the world. A hummingbird nest has only enough room for two tiny eggs and one parent. Eagle nests are very large. One eagle nest can weigh up to 1 ton (0.9 tonnes).

◼ **Birds build nests in water, on the ground, in trees, and on cliffs.**

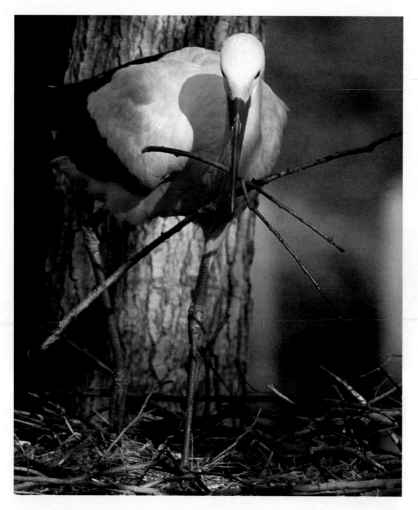

Nests can be made from different materials. Anything a bird can carry might end up in a nest. Feathers, fur, grass, and moss all help to make nests. Some nests are made from mud. Birds will even add bits of garbage, such as tin foil or string, to their nests.

Different Types of Nests

Ovenbirds make their nests out of clay and mud. It takes thousands of trips for the birds to carry the mud to the nest. The nests look like small clay ovens.

Some birds let other birds do their work. Cowbirds lay their eggs in the nest of another type of bird. The other bird will care for the eggs and even feed the young birds after they hatch.

Woodpeckers make a nest inside hollow areas in tree trunks.

Weaver birds live in Africa. The male birds use their beaks to weave round nests in trees. They sit in the nest's entrance and flap their wings to attract female birds.

Activity

Spot a Bird's Nest

Next time you go outdoors, look up into the trees to see if you can spot a nest. If you see bits of dried grass or twigs in a tree, it could be a nest. Larger nests, such as those made by crows, are usually easy to see.

Web of Life

All living things depend on other living things to survive. Every plant and animal has its place in nature. If humans do not interfere with nature, the environment stays in balance. A food chain shows how animals survive by eating plants or other animals. Energy is transferred from one living thing to another in a food chain. When many food chains are connected, it is called a food web.

Birds play a very important role in a food web. They eat insects that we consider pests. Some birds eat small mammals that disturb farmers.

■ **American robins often eat worms.**

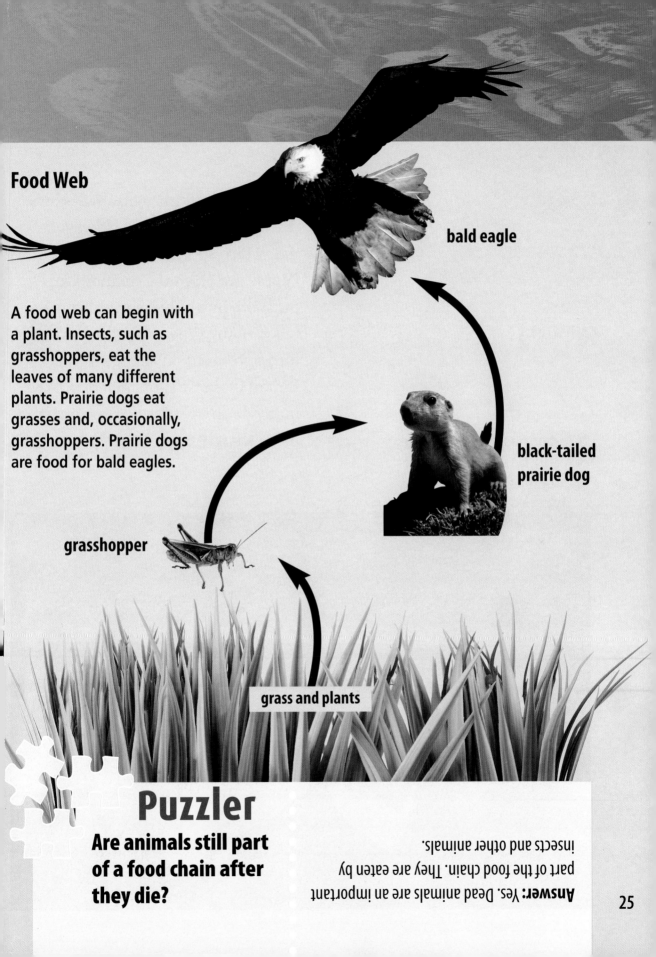

Food Web

bald eagle

A food web can begin with a plant. Insects, such as grasshoppers, eat the leaves of many different plants. Prairie dogs eat grasses and, occasionally, grasshoppers. Prairie dogs are food for bald eagles.

black-tailed prairie dog

grasshopper

grass and plants

Puzzler

Are animals still part of a food chain after they die?

Answer: Yes. Dead animals are an important part of the food chain. They are eaten by insects and other animals.

Protecting Birds

Hopefully, birds will always be a part of our world. However, many bird species are endangered. People are often the main reason birds are in trouble, since they have killed many types of birds. The dodo bird once lived on islands in the Indian Ocean. Sailors killed and ate many dodos. Dodos became **extinct** more than three hundred years ago.

■ Today, passenger pigeons can only be seen in natural history museums.

The passenger pigeon is also extinct. At one time, millions of passenger pigeons flew in the skies. People took over forest land to build homes and towns. The pigeons had nowhere to live. Humans also hunted the wild pigeons extensively. The last passenger pigeon died in **captivity** in the Cincinnati Zoo in 1914.

Today, most people are trying to save endangered birds. For example, bald eagles are threatened because of the large numbers killed by hunters and trappers. Pollution and the rapid growth of farms and cities have contributed to the loss of their habitat.

■ Pollution nearly destroyed peregrine falcons. Scientists worked to help captive peregrines lay eggs. The new birds were then released into nature.

Puzzler

Chopping down trees in a forest can endanger birds. Why?

Answer: Birds build nests in the trees in a forest. They eat plants and insects that live in the forest. Without trees, the birds lose their homes.

27

Singing is for the Birds

We often hear birds singing even if we cannot see them. Bird sounds can be beautiful and distinctive. Many birds talk to one another through songs or calls. Birds have different sounding calls that mean different things. A bird may sing in order to attract a mate. It may send a message that it is in the area. Birds that live in **flocks** often make calls to warn other birds of danger.

■ Flocks of red-winged blackbirds sing their song repeatedly.

Bird-watchers listen to bird songs. Bird calls can help them locate a bird. Bird-watchers can tell what type of birds are in the area by their sounds. A scientist or bird-watcher may play a recording of certain bird sounds in order to attract birds.

■ The chickadee sounds like it is saying its own name when it sings. Its song sounds like *chick-a-dee-dee-dee.*

Puzzler
Why do many birds sing mostly during the day?

Answer: Many birds may be resting or sleeping during the night. Birds remain quiet so they will not be heard by **predators** that are out at night looking for food.

The First Bird

Scientists believe birds developed from reptiles. Feathers may have originally been scales. Flying reptiles called pterosaurs lived alongside the dinosaurs. Flying reptiles did not have feathers. Their wings were covered by skin, similar to bats' wings. Pterosaurs died out with the dinosaurs.

■ **Crocodiles (pictured) and alligators are the closest living relatives to birds.**

Birds are not related to these animals. The first-known bird lived more than 130 million years ago. **Fossils** of this animal, called Archaeopteryx, show that it was the first animal to have feathers. Archaeopteryx was about the size of a crow. Like reptiles, it had teeth and a tail.

■ Crows are about 20 inches (51 centimeters) long.

Puzzler

Archaeopteryx had scales on its legs and a bony tail. Do birds have these features today?

Answer: No. Birds have only feathers, not scales like reptiles. Birds' tails are made of feathers only, not of bone.

Glossary

albumen: the clear or white inside part of an egg

amphibians: animals that live in water and on land

camouflage: to blend in with the colors of the environment in order to stay hidden from danger

captivity: to be kept away from natural habitat; confined

endangered: at risk of dying out completely

extinct: no longer in existence

flocks: groups of birds

fossils: the remains of plants or animals found hardened in layers of rock

habitats: environments in which birds live

nectar: a sweet liquid in many flowers

poultry: birds, such as chickens and turkeys, kept for meat and eggs

predators: animals that search out and eat other animals

preening: when a bird uses its beak as a comb to keep its feathers clean and healthy

prey: animals that are eaten by other animals

reproduce: to produce young

species: a group of closely-related animals or plants that are often similar in behavior and appearance

yolk: the yellow inside part of an egg

Index

adapt 18, 19
albumen 15

barbs 17
barbules 17
bills 4, 8, 9
bird-watchers 13, 14, 29

camouflage 20, 21
captive 27

down 15, 16

eggs 4, 6, 7, 15, 18, 21, 22, 23, 27
endangered 13, 26, 27
extinct 26, 27

feathers 5, 7, 11, 15, 16, 17, 18, 19, 22, 30, 31
flock 28
food chain 24, 25
food web 24, 25
fossils 31

habitat 10, 11, 18, 27

life cycle 6

nests 6, 7, 11, 18, 20, 21, 22, 23, 27

ornithology 12, 13

poultry 12, 13
predators 29
preening 17
prey 8, 9, 10, 18, 21

reproduce 6

shaft (feather) 17
songs 28, 29
species 4, 10, 20, 26

Ukrainian Easter eggs 15

vane 17

yolk 15

Websites

www.enchantedlearning.com/subjects/birds
http://nationalzoo.si.edu/Animals/Birds
www.birds.cornell.edu
www.audubon.org

Some websites stay current longer than others. For further websites, use your search engines to locate topics such as bird-watching, hummingbirds, parrots, and pets.